A Day in the Life: Desert Animals

Fennec Fox

Anita Ganeri

www.raintreepublishers.co.uk
Visit our website to find out
more information about
Raintree books.

To order:

☎ Phone 0845 6044371

🖻 Fax +44 (0) 1865 312263

✉ Email myorders@raintreepublishers.co.uk

Customers from outside the UK please telephone +44 1865 312262

Raintree is an imprint of Capstone Global Library Limited,
a company incorporated in England and Wales having
its registered office at 7 Pilgrim Street, London, EC4V 6LB
– Registered company number: 6695582

Text © Capstone Global Library Limited 2011
First published in hardback in 2011
The moral rights of the proprietor have been asserted.

Edited by Daniel Nunn, Rebecca Rissman, and Sian Smith
Designed by Richard Parker
Picture research by Elizabeth Alexander
Production by Victoria Fitzgerald
Originated by Capstone Global Library Ltd
Printed and bound in China by South China Printing
Company Ltd

ISBN 978 1 406 21961 6 (hardback)
14 13 12 11 10
10 9 8 7 6 5 4 3 2 1

British Library Cataloguing in Publication Data

Ganeri, Anita, 1961-
Fennec fox. -- (A day in the life. Desert animals)
1. Fennec--Juvenile literature.
I. Title II. Series
599.7'76-dc22

Acknowledgements

We would like to thank the following for permission to
reproduce photographs: Alamy pp. 4, 15, 23 glossary
mammal (© blickwinkel), 5 (© Juniors Bildarchiv), 17, 23
glossary burrow, 23 glossary dune (© INTERFOTO); FLPA
pp. 8 (© David Hosking), 20, 23 glossary cub (© Yossi
Eshbol), 14 (© Mandal Ranjit); Getty Images pp. 9, 16
(© 2007 Kim in cherl); iStockphoto p. 18 (© Alan Hewitt);
Nature Picture Library pp. 21, 23 glossary predator (James
Aldred); Photolibrary pp. 10, 13, 19 (Eyal Bartov/OSF),
12 (Simon Murrell/Imagestate), 22 (Juniors Bildarchiv);
Shutterstock pp. 7, 23 glossary desert (© Nuno Miguel
Duarte Rodrigues Lopes), 23 glossary insect (© Richard
Williamson), 23 glossary grasshopper (© Anke van Wyk);
Still Pictures p. 11 (John Cancalosi/Peter Arnold).

Front cover photograph of a fennec fox (Vulpes zerda) in
the Sahara Desert, Algeria reproduced with permission of
Corbis (© Frans Lemmens).

Back cover photograph of (left) a fennec fox asleep
reproduced with permission of iStockphoto (© Alan Hewitt);
and (right) four young fennec fox cubs reproduced with
permission of FLPA (© Yossi Eshbol).

We would like to thank Michael Bright for his assistance in
the preparation of this book.

Contents

Some words are shown in bold, **like this**.
You can find them in the glossary on page 23.

What is a fennec fox?

A fennec fox is a **mammal**.

All mammals have some hair on their bodies and feed their babies milk.

Fennec foxes are the smallest foxes.

This adult fennec fox is about the same size as a pet cat.

Where do fennec foxes live?

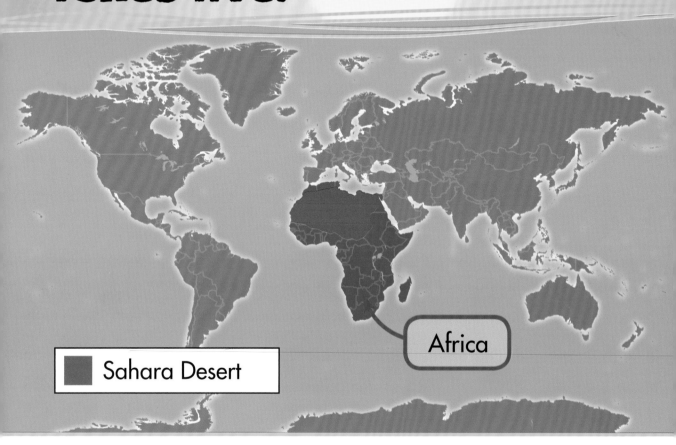

Africa

| | Sahara Desert |

Most fennec foxes live in the Sahara **Desert** in North Africa.

Can you find this desert on the map?

sand dune

The desert is hot in the day and cold at night, with very little rain.

Fennec foxes live in **burrows** among the **sand dunes**.

What do fennec foxes look like?

tail

Fennec foxes are small, with long, bushy tails.

They have thick, sand-coloured fur.

Fennec foxes have big ears to help them hear and keep cool.

Their feet are furry for walking across hot sand without getting burned.

What do fennec foxes do at night?

burrow

At night, foxes come out of their **burrows** to hunt for food.

Their fur coats help to keep them warm.

A fox uses its big ears to find food in the dark.

It listens out for the sound of its **prey** moving about.

What do fennec foxes eat?

grasshopper

Fennec foxes mostly hunt **desert insects**, such as grasshoppers and locusts.

They also eat mice, lizards, birds, and eggs.

The foxes do not need to drink water.

They get all the water they need from the food they eat.

What hunts fennec foxes?

hyena

A fox has to listen out for night-time hunters, such as hyenas.

If there is danger, a fox runs back to its **burrow**.

eagle owl

Eagle owls also hunt and eat fennec foxes.

Some people hunt fennec foxes for their meat and fur, or to keep them as pets.

Do fennec foxes live in groups?

Fennec foxes hunt on their own at night.

But the rest of the time, they live in family groups of up to ten foxes.

sand dune

burrow

A family of foxes lives together in a **burrow** deep inside the **sand dunes**.

The foxes dig their burrows with their feet.

What do fennec foxes do in the day?

In the day, it is very hot in the **desert**.

The foxes sleep in their **burrows** where it is cooler.

If a fox goes outside, its sand-coloured fur helps to hide it from **predators**.

Its huge ears give off heat to help it keep cool.

What are baby fennec foxes called?

Baby fennec foxes are called **cubs**.

Their eyes open about ten days after they are born.

The female stays in the **burrow** with the cubs.

The male guards the burrow from **predators** and brings food for the cubs.

Fennec fox body map

ears

tail

fur

eye

mouth

feet

whiskers

Glossary

 **burrow** hole in the ground where a fennec fox lives

 **cub** young or baby fox

 **desert** very dry place that is rocky, stony, or sandy

 **insect** animal that has six legs, such as a grasshopper or an ant

 **mammal** animal that feeds its babies milk. All mammals have some hair or fur on their bodies.

 **predator** animal that hunts other animals for food

 **prey** animal that is eaten by other animals

 **sand dune** big pile of sand blown into a heap by the wind

Find out more

Books

Desert Animals (Focus on Habitats), Stephen Savage (Wayland, 2006)

Deserts (My World of Geography), Angela Royston (Heinemann Library, 2004)

24 Hours: Desert (Focus on Habitats), Elizabeth Haldane (Dorling Kindersley, 2006)

Websites

Learn more about fennec foxes at:
kids.nationalgeographic.com/kids/animals/creaturefeature/fennec-foxes

Look at lots of videos and pictures of fennec foxes at:
www.arkive.org/fennec-fox/vulpes-zerda

Index